MICHELANGELO

Mason Crest Publishers, Inc.
370 Reed Road
Broomall, Pennsylvania 19008
866-MCP-BOOK (toll free)

Illustrations copyright © 2001
Art Ageence "PIART"
Published in association with
Grimm Press Ltd., Taiwan
Printed in Taiwan.
1 3 5 7 9 8 6 4 2

Library of Congress Cataloging-in-Publication Data:

on file at the Library of Congress.

ISBN 1-59084-160-3
ISBN 1-59084-133-6 (series)

Great Names

MICHELANGELO

On the evening of March 6, 1475, a baby boy was born in Florence to Lobodvico di Buonarroti Simoni, an old aristocratic Florentine family, who named him Michelangelo di Buonarotti Simoni. It was a prophetic name, for this child was indeed like an angel who came to spread beauty.

Michelangelo was the second of five children. His mother died when he was six, and Michelangelo lived for several years with his nurse in the country. Near her house was a quarry where stonemasons and sculptors worked. Michelangelo loved it there. To him, the sound of chisels was music and the sight of the marble mysteriously inviting. "If my brain really is better than other people's, it is because I breathed clean air and milk and marble dust as I grew up."

When he returned to Florence, Michelangelo was sent to school. In classes he was always drawing, filling the margins of his books with sketches. One day he summoned the courage to tell his father he wanted to be an artist.

"Artists are manual workers, hardly better than cobblers," replied his father angrily. "We're nobles, not laborers! The answer is no! I won't allow it."

Michelangelo tried to think of something that would persuade his father. "If I enter Domenico Ghirlandaio's studio, he will pay me," he said, having no idea whether this was true or not. His father finally agreed that he would enter Domenico Ghirlandaio's workshop for three years for a wage of 24 gold ducats.

In the workshop, Michelangelo studied very hard. Unlike other students, he didn't just copy works of his master. He also went off on his own to copy the great Giotto and Masaccio murals. The line and light of these old masterpieces taught him as much as a living teacher. By copying them, he learned their techniques. In spite of his youth, his style was very mature and so accomplished that when he deliberately "antiqued" some copies he had made, they were mistaken for the work of a great master.

Once, observing a fellow student copying a work of their master, he took the original, quickly redrew one of the figures, and altered the lighting. The effect was immediate. Ghirlandaio was amazed and a little jealous of Michelangelo's talent. Though only in his teens, the boy already had the confidence to alter his teacher's work. A year later, Michelangelo entered Lorenzo de Medici's Garden.

Lorenzo's Garden belonged to Lorenzo the Magnificent. It housed his collection of large sculptures and was a place where young artists could study and learn to sculpture. Michelangelo was deeply affected by what he saw in the garden. He was amazed at how the hard stone became soft, smooth flesh and how completely perfect the statues looked, despite the fact that most were damaged. Captivated, Michelangelo copied these ancient statues. His work, which closely resembled the originals, impressed Lorenzo so much that he took a special interest in the boy and offered him a place in his own home. Michelangelo's father was pleased. He hadn't expected anything good to come from Michelangelo's desire to become an artist.

Michelangelo went to live in the vast Medici residence where he was treated as part of the family. He was given an allowance of five ducats a week. Here he met many of the most important intellectual and cultural figures of the day and was introduced to the latest literary and philosophical ideas. He grew friendly with the younger generation of Medicis, two of whom later became popes: Pope Leo X and Pope Clement VII.

His extraordinary talent meant his work was much better than his fellow students. Sometimes, in his arrogance, he hurt their feelings. On one occasion, when the class was copying a Masaccio mural, Michelangelo ridiculed the others' technique so much that his friend, Torigiano, exploded in anger and punched him in the nose.

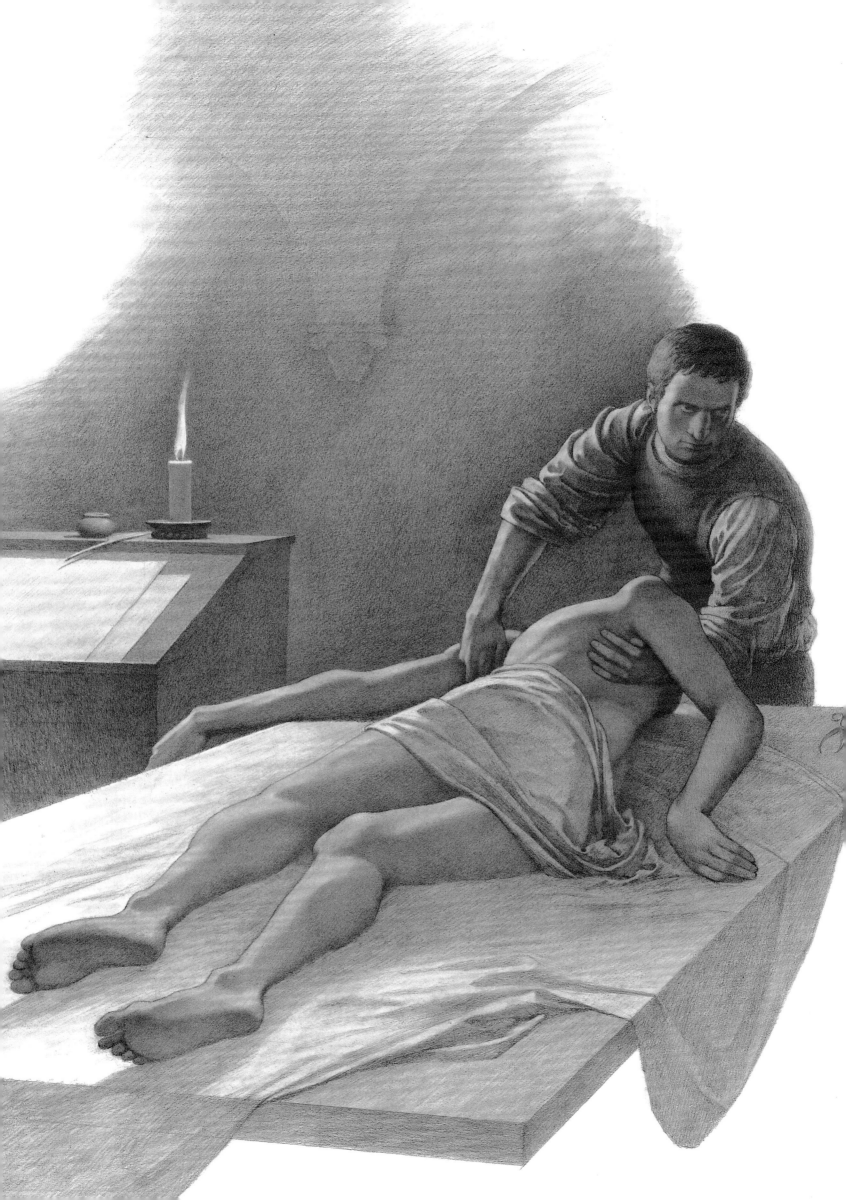

But copying the works of others was not enough to satisfy Michelangelo's thirst for knowledge. He knew that to produce a great sculpture he had to first understand the structure of the human body, so he asked the head of the church of Santo Spirito for permission to dissect the dead bodies as they lay in the church. He was told he must do so in absolute secrecy. To thank the abbot for his help, he carved him a crucifix.

During this period, Michelangelo often spent evenings alone in the dark church examining bodies, turning them this way and that until he had worked out the arrangement of the muscles, blood vessels, and skeleton. He sketched everything he observed, often working right through until dawn. His family began to worry about his behavior, but he could not tell them the real reason for his absences. If he had, they would have probably worried more than before.

Michelangelo produced two sculptures during this time, *Madonna of the Stairs* and *Battle of the Centaurs*.

When Michelangelo finished his work *Sleeping Cupid*, one of his acquaintances said to him, "If you were to prepare it so that it would appear to have been buried, it would pass for an antique. You could then sell it for a lot more money."

Michelangelo did this and the work was sold to Cardinal San Giogrio. The truth soon came out, however, and the cardinal was naturally furious. But the incident made Michelangelo famous throughout Rome. When he was 21, he was called to work for the church.

Since the Pope didn't know much about art, Michelangelo wasn't given any work to do at first. But he wasn't idle. The city was full of ancient, recently unearthed statues and ruins. He spent his time studying and sketching these wonderful examples of classical art. He also produced a number of large sculptures. Based on the exemplary sculptures, he soon received a commission from one of the cardinals to create the Vatican Pietà.

It took Michelangelo two years to complete this sculpture, in which a beautifully proportioned body of the dead Christ lies in the arms of a mourning Madonna. It was a tremendous triumph for Michelangelo, surpassing the classical style both in terms of composition and expression. It was as though the figures were not carved at all, but lived in the stone and had simply been revealed in form and in spirit by the sculptor.

After the Vatican Pietà was displayed in St. Peter's, Michelangelo overheard a crowd of pilgrims from Lombardy discussing it.

"Who carved this?" one asked. "I heard it was Christoforo Solari," replied another.

Michelangelo left without saying anything, but the next day one of the church administrators discovered a sash draped around the statue with the words,

"Michelangelo Buonarroti, Florence, made this." This was his first famous sculpture. He was 25 years old.

Soon after this, he received some news that made him hurry back to Florence. For several years, he had his eye on a huge piece of stone about 20 feet (6 meters) tall. A sculptor had ruined the stone by cutting a big hole through the base. It was left in a church, but now there was talk about using it again.

Michelangelo fought to be allowed to carve the stone. He eventually won. Many sculptors thought it would be impossible to carve a complete human figure from it because it was so badly damaged, but Michelangelo wanted to try. Florence had just emerged from war and established a republic. The new government commissioned him to make a statue of David, a symbol of freedom.

He examined the stone from all angles and, as he did so, the figure of David slowly started taking shape in his mind. In the Bible, David is a liberator. Michelangelo wanted his David to symbolize the power of the people and to inspire confidence. He also wanted to convey the idea that only men as just and as brave as David were fit to rule Florence.

He made sketches of David in all poses that were possible given the existing hole. Then he set up scaffolding around the stone and walled off the area. This was now his studio and no one was allowed into it until the work was finished.

Three years later, *David* was complete. He was perfect, melding strength and beauty, scale and detail, in a way never seen before. Michelangelo insisted that the work by placed in the Plazza Vecchio so that all the people of Florence could see it. But there was a problem. They had to figure out how to get it there.

More than 13 feet (4 meters) high and made of marble, *David* was obviously extremely heavy. An architect was called in to construct a special wooden frame from which *David* was to be hung with ropes. The ropes were tied with a special kind of slipknot, invented by Michelangelo. They got tighter and tighter the more weight there was on them. Four men took five days to move *David* from the church to the square.

People packed the square to look at the new statue, but not everyone liked what they saw—a naked man standing out in the open—and some threw stones at it. Gradually, however people began to appreciate the statue and to see that Michelangelo had given them a great and inspiring symbol. From then on his name, like his statue, soared above Florence.

The first prime minister of the new Republic of Florence, Pier Soderini, was very pleased with *David*, but he had one reservation. Wasn't the nose a little too broad? Michelangelo noted that the prime minister was standing right beneath the nose when he asked this question and therefore could not see whether the proportions were right or not. Nevertheless, in order to appease the great man, Michelangelo took up a handful of marble chips, grabbed his hammer and chisel, and climbed up the scaffold. Once he reached the head, he pretended to chip away at the nose, dropping a few of the marble chips from time to time. After a while he called down to the prime minister, "How's that?"

"Much better," the prime minister replied. "That's brought him to life!" Michelangelo climbed down, laughing to himself about how silly this man was. He knew nothing about art but thought he knew everything.

An art collector friend of Michelangelo's, Agnolo Doni, wanted to buy a work from him, and so Michelangelo painted *The Dono Tondo*. This is the only painting Michelangelo ever did that was not on a wall or ceiling. When the work was finished, Michelangelo wrapped it in paper, wrote a request for 70 gold ducats, and sent it off. Agnolo Doni wasn't prepared to pay that amount, however, even though he knew the work was worth much more. He sent back 40.

Michelangelo immediately returned this money with the message: "If Agnolo doesn't pay me a 100 pieces of gold, then I want the painting back." Agnolo liked the painting very much. He was not prepared to pay the new price either, so he sent back the 70 gold ducats originally requested. This made Michelangelo doubly angry.

"Still trying to bargain? The price is now double: 140 pieces of gold! And if he doesn't pay up, bring the painting back immediately!"

Realizing the situation had gotten out of hand, Agnolo paid.

In 1503, Julius II was named Pope. As soon as he took up his post, he commissioned Michelangelo, who was 27, to begin work on his tomb. He wanted to use Michelangelo's genius to secure himself a place in history. Michelangelo quickly drew up a plan that was not only accepted by Julius II, but also stirred his greater ambitions. He decided to completely renovate St. Peter's Basilica and place his tomb within it.

Greatly encouraged and full of expectation, Michelangelo set to work. Taking several assistants with him, he went to Carrara to select the stones to be used, and remained there for eight months, soaking up inspiration from the stone and the environment.

The selected stones were loaded onto boats for the trip to Rome, but unexpected flooding of the Tiber River delayed their departure for some time. When the stones finally made it to Rome, Julius II, engrossed with the rebuilding of St. Peter's and short of money, failed to pay the shippers as agreed. Michelangelo went to talk to him but was told the Pope was too busy to see him. Furious, Michelangelo left the city the same night for Florence. As soon as the Pope heard of this, he sent five men after him, but Michelangelo refused to return.

In Florence, Michelangelo began work on a mural for the Council Hall. Three times the Pope sent orders for him to return to Rome, but Michelangelo ignored them until Pier Sodieri persuaded him to go to Bologna where the Pope was visiting. Michelangelo entered and knelt before him. The Pope, who was almost angry, glared at him with half-real anger and said, "So, you've waited until I came to you."

With gifts and promises, the Pope got Michelangelo to return to Rome. Instead of asking him to continue work on the tomb, the Pope ordered him to make a bronze statue. The delay was fatal—Michelangelo never managed to finish the tomb.

While Julius II was alive, Michelangelo only finished four of the 40 statues proposed for the tomb. He started working on another eight of the 40. This project became his biggest headache during the 40 years between its beginning and his death.

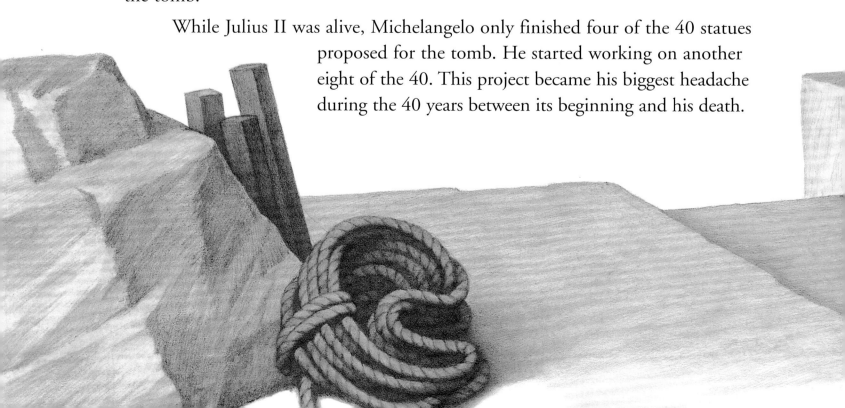

Julius II was loud in his praise of Michelangelo's talent and this made many other artists jealous. The leading architect of the day, Donato Bramante, was a relative and friend of the young painter Raphael. He convinced the Pope that it was bad luck to build his tomb while he still lived and that he should stop the project and ask Michelangelo to paint the Sistine Chapel instead. Since Michelangelo had never painted a mural, Bramante believed he was bound to fail. When Michelangelo failed to finish the project, it would be possible for Raphael to replace him as the Pope's favorite.

Michelangelo told the Pope he did not want to paint the mural because he was a sculptor and knew little about painting. But the more he tried to refuse, the more the Pope insisted, leaving him no choice but to accept. Ordered by the Pope to prepare everything so Michelangelo could start painting, Bramante hung platforms on ropes from the ceiling. When asked how the ceiling would be repaired at the end, he replied casually, "We'll think of something when the time comes. What else can we do?"

Michelangelo, who realized that Bramante was either an idiot or deliberately trying to undermine him, complained to the Pope, who replied, "Do it your own way then." So Michelangelo designed and built an arched platform and supported it by using existing apertures above the cornice. He gave the unneeded rope to one of his carpenters, who received enough money from its sale to fund his daughter's dowry.

Michelangelo completed his design for the ceiling and then went to Florence to seek the help and advice of painters. They demonstrated to him all the different painting

techniques, but none of them achieved the effect he wanted.
"Painting is not just line and light," he thought. One night, almost crazy with despair and frustration, he scrapped everything he had done and started again. He also worked locked away behind closed doors, allowing no one to see what he was doing.

Michelangelo carried out his massive project more or less by himself. Although he had a few assistants, he supervised everything they did. He worked 15 or more hours a day and often slept fully clothed on the platform. It was extremely uncomfortable, tiring work. It was lonely too since no one could enter, not even the Pope. He wrote a poem describing the experience:

This comes from dangling from the ceiling—
I'm goitered like a Lombard cat (or wherever else their throats grow fat)—
It's my belly that's beyond concealing,
It hangs beneath my chin like peeling.
My beard points skyward,
I seem like a bat upon its back, I've breast and splat!
On my face, the paint's congealing.
Loins concertina'd in my gut
I drop my butt as counterweight and move without the help of eyes.
Like a skinned martyr I abut on air, and wrinkled show my fate.
Bow-like, I strain towards the skies.
No wonder then I size things crookedly; I'm on all fours
Bent blowpipes send their darts off-course.
Defend my labor's cause,
Good Giovanni, from all strictures:
I live in hell and paint its pictures.

When the first half of the ceiling was finished, the Pope announced eagerly that he wanted to be the first to see it. He couldn't wait for the platform to be moved away or the rubbish to be removed. The curtain was drawn away to reveal a sight so majestic it flooded the room. Michelangelo had applied the techniques of sculpture to painting, creating huge, lifelike figures that filled the air, joyous, angry, moving, still, enacting the age-old story of the creation and drawing sighs of amazement from the viewers.

The second part of the ceiling
took another year to complete. The impatient Pope
asked so often about when it would be finished that Michelangelo snapped,
"It will be finished when I've finished."

The angry Pope banged his staff on the ground and shouted, "What
do you mean by it will be finished when you've finished? Stop wasting time
and get on with it or I'll throw you off the platform!"

On the morning of All Saint's Day 1512, Julius II said mass in the
Sistine Chapel and the ceiling was unveiled to the people of Rome. They
were the first to see a masterpiece that surpassed anything that had been
done before, a masterpiece whose fame, and that of its creator, would live
on forever.

"After four tortured years and over 400 more than life-sized figures,
I felt as old and weary as Jeremiah. I was only 37, yet friends did not
recognize the old man I had become."

When Julius II died, the popes that followed him kept Michelangelo busy with work and little time to devote to the tomb of Julius II. His unfulfilled promise to complete the tomb became a problem that troubled him for the rest of his life.

In 1526, France invaded Rome and a revolt broke out in Florence. The Medici family was driven out of Florence, and a new government installed. It was decided to modernize the fortifications around the city and appoint Michelangelo as the project's supervisor. He was now 52.

After surveying the city, Michelangelo drew up a plan, and work commenced at several sites throughout the city. The most unique element of his plan was the design and construction, from his own chosen materials (chestnut, oak, and unfired mud bricks), of a crab-shaped bastion on the hill of St. Miniato. It took about six months for this bastion to be built. Michelangelo supervised the work constantly. If the bastion was taken by invaders, the whole city would fall.

Three years later, Florence was surrounded. Michelangelo was sent to strengthen the fortifications and was appointed one of nine members of the military council. But when the enemy blockaded the city, Michelangelo realized there was nothing more he could do. He left Florence.

When the war was over, Michelangelo returned to Florence. By now he didn't have the strength or time to do everything by himself, so he began to work with a team of assistants. Despite their help, there was always more work than he could hope to complete, a problem made worse by the fact that he destroyed any work that did not meet his high standards. He lived and worked under immense pressure, like a slave. "Day and night, I don't dare think about anything except work," he said.

In 1533 Pope Clement VII asked him to paint *The Last Judgment* in the Sistine Chapel. At the time, the business of Julius II's unfinished tomb was causing Michelangelo problems again. Julius II's nephew had accused him of accepting the payment of 16,000 silver ducats but not completing the work. After much negotiation, the two parties agreed to reduce the scale of the project and to continue to work on it at the same time as the Sistine Chapel mural.

A year later, Pope Clement VII died, and Michelangelo thought he would at last be able to give all his attention to Julius II's tomb. But the new pope, Pope Paul III, called him and said, "I have waited 30 years to be pope and now that I am, I want you to stay here and work for me, regardless of what previous arrangements you might have." He then ordered Michelangelo to continue his work on *The Last Judgment.* Michaelangelo was now 60 years old.

On one of the Pope's visits to see how *The Last Judgment* was getting on, one of his attendants, Biagna da Cesena, said, "It's indecent to have so many naked bodies in a sacred place like this. They are better fit for a public bathhouse or a bar!"

This infuriated Michelangelo. As soon as they left, he painted da Cesena as Minos, the supreme judge of the underworld. No matter how much da Cesena pleaded with him, Michelangelo refused to alter it. Da Cesena then went to the Pope, who joked, "If Michelangelo had put you in purgatory, I could help you. But he has painted you in hell. There's nothing I can do! No one can help you once you're in hell."

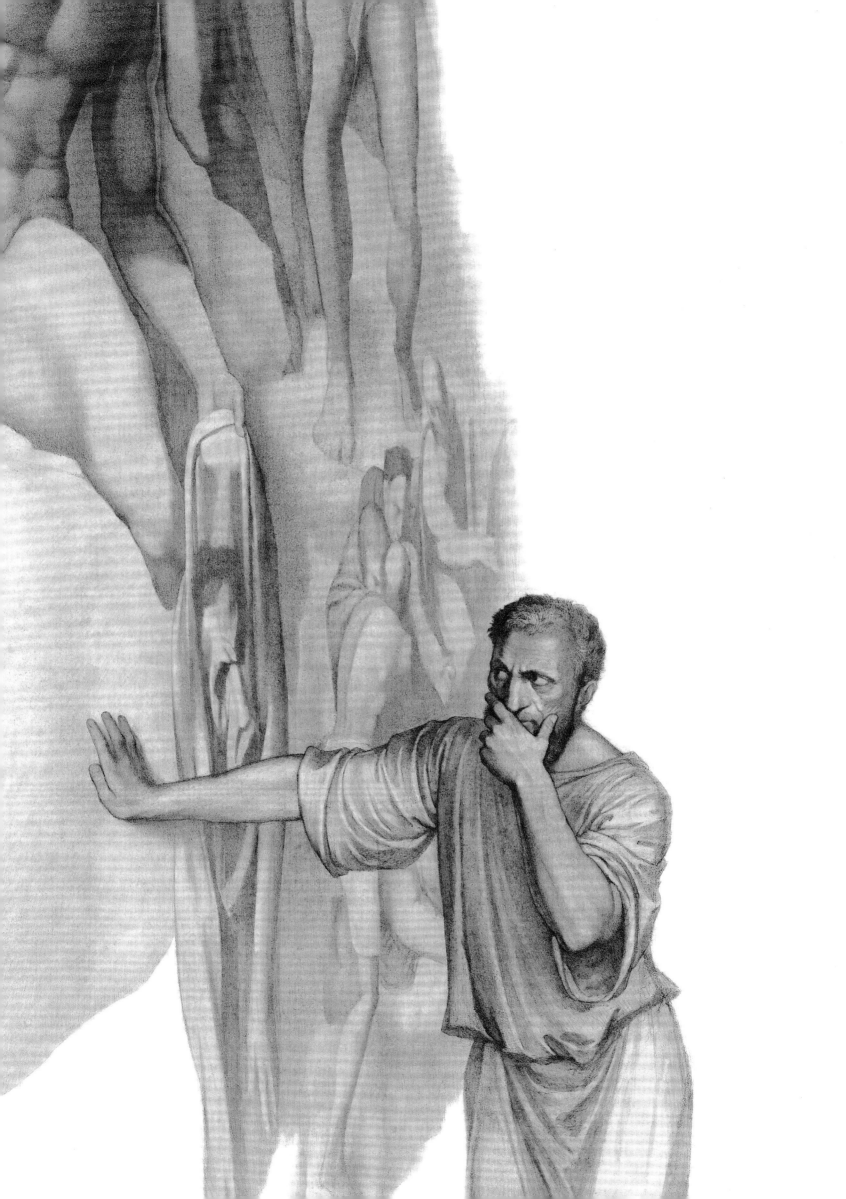

The Church wanted St. Peter's Cathedral to be so great that it would outshine the monuments of ancient Rome.

In 1546, the man responsible for the rebuilding of St. Peter's Cathedral, Antonio da Sangallo, died and the Pope asked Michelangelo to take over the project. Michelangelo was 72. He knew it would probably be his last work.

Michelangelo threw himself into the project, making huge changes to da Sangallo's design. He ordered the workers to work, work, work! He personally calculated every beam and attended to every detail.

As in the past, others were jealous of his genius, and he had to deal with rumor, slander, and plots against him. His enemies said his eyesight was poor and his brain muddled, but Michelangelo did not give in. Old and ill, he continued to struggle on until the very end.

Today, no one can look at the magnificent St. Peter's Cathedral without a feeling of awe and respect. Michelangelo used the last of his spirit and energy to create this sacred hall. When we gasp in admiration at its murals, its sculpture, and its architecture, we are really gasping in praise of an extraordinary genius.

The popes hoped to use his talent to be sure that history remembered them, but the name that is remembered today is Michelangelo.

BIOGRAPHY

Author Diane Cook is a journalist and freelance writer. She has written hundreds of newspaper articles and writes regularly for national magazines, trade publications, and web sites. She lives in Dover, Delaware, with her husband and three children.